Francisco Werlen da Silva Taveira
Jalil Castro Dray
Lena Andrea Lima Muniz

Materials Logistics:

AF154851

Francisco Werlen da Silva Taveira
Jalil Castro Dray
Lena Andrea Lima Muniz

Materials Logistics:

A study at the Port of Parintins - AM

ScienciaScripts

Imprint

Any brand names and product names mentioned in this book are subject to trademark, brand or patent protection and are trademarks or registered trademarks of their respective holders. The use of brand names, product names, common names, trade names, product descriptions etc. even without a particular marking in this work is in no way to be construed to mean that such names may be regarded as unrestricted in respect of trademark and brand protection legislation and could thus be used by anyone.

Cover image: www.ingimage.com

This book is a translation from the original published under ISBN 978-620-2-19301-6.

Publisher:
Sciencia Scripts
is a trademark of
Dodo Books Indian Ocean Ltd. and OmniScriptum S.R.L publishing group

120 High Road, East Finchley, London, N2 9ED, United Kingdom
Str. Armeneasca 28/1, office 1, Chisinau MD-2012, Republic of Moldova, Europe
Printed at: see last page
ISBN: 978-620-7-26888-7

INDICE

Summary

The main objective of today's freight transport scenario is to meet the needs of customers in terms of time, cost, information and quality, and one of the modes of transport that is a benchmark worldwide in terms of customer satisfaction is water transport. The process in the distribution chain that deserves a lot of attention is the movement of the goods being transported, as it is the stage in this whole process where we add quality to the service provided. In Brazil, and specifically in the state of Amazonas, there is a greater incidence of river transport due to the fact that there is a rich and extensive waterway potential in the region in question, as well as the absence of other modes of transport. In this context, the municipality of Parintins is located in the interior of the state, as it is an island and the city is restricted to just two modes of transport, river and air. Because it is the most economical mode of transport and the most feasible for the municipality, companies opt for river transportation to obtain and transport their goods. The boats that carry out the Parintins/Manaus/Parintins stretch are very competitive in the market, with seven boats from the municipality and another twenty-one from neighboring municipalities making connections in Parintins. Therefore, the existence of strategic differentials in the companies that manage these boats is essential, not just in terms of price, but above all in terms of the quality of the services they provide, which are the *sine qua non* conditions for the survival of companies in highly competitive environments. With this in mind, this research aims to investigate and highlight the processes and methods used in the movement of materials by ship in the port of Parintins.

From the results of the survey, it was possible to conclude that the municipality's boats invest in quality and speed of service, because even though they are still carried out in an anachronistic way, this is in line with the municipality's demand for this activity.

Keywords: *Transportation Logistics; Material Handling; Port of Parintins.*

INTRODUCTION

The transportation of goods in the Amazon region takes place mostly by river, both because of the lack of other viable modes of transportation in the region and because of its great waterway potential, given the existence of the Amazon basin, the largest hydrographic basin in terms of length and volume of water in the world, allowing river transportation to be the most economically viable form of transportation for the region in question.

Waterway transportation is the subject of much discussion not only in the region in question, but throughout Brazil. The fact that it is the most economically viable way of transporting cargo means that it meets all of Novaes' (2004, p. 145) precepts about physical distribution: "the general objective of physical distribution, as an ideal goal, is to get the right products to the right places at the right time, with the desired level of service and at the lowest possible price".

According to Soares (2012), transportation is of the utmost importance in reducing a company's logistics costs, since its elements represent between 33.3% and 66.6% of total logistics costs, an understanding also consolidated by Rosa (2007, p. 27), who states that "logistics costs are a key factor in stimulating trade". Therefore, the importance of balancing logistics costs in reducing organizational expenses and mitigating the operating costs of the entire supply chain can be seen. The movement of materials is part of this context of transport and yogic costs, as well as being a factor that adds satisfaction to the end customer, as Silva et al. (2013, p. 3) point out "[...] the movement of materials becomes a strategic part of the organization's business, so that this effort can somehow be converted into a competitive advantage, either in terms of cost reduction or by increasing customer satisfaction".

Located in the far east of the state of Amazonas, on the border with the state of Parà, is the municipality of Parintins, which, due to its location on the banks of the Amazon River, one of the main waterways in the Amazon region, has great strategic potential for transporting goods.

Parintins has a working port, managed by the Administraçâo das Hidrovias da Amazônia Ocidental (AHIMOC), a federal authority linked to the Ministry of Transport, with an area of 7. 675 m and an appropriate physical space for receiving and distributing goods.675 m^2 and an appropriate physical space for receiving and distributing goods, but even though it is the second largest waterway terminal in Amazonas, constantly receiving tourist ships and regional vessels, this activity is partially carried out at the port (CAVALCANTE; FONTINELLY; ROCHA, 2012).

The aim of this study is to investigate the process of moving materials from ships in the port of the municipality of Parintins, with a view to understanding some aspects of this process, such as the packaging of goods on these ships, the turnover of the companies operating in the port of Parintins with this activity, the difficulties encountered in carrying out this service and, finally, to try to understand the reason for the partial operation of the port of Parintins.

METHODOLOGY

In order to present the movement of materials by vessels in the port of the municipality of Parintins, the research is classified by Vergara (2000) as descriptive, because it exposes the characteristics of a population or phenomenon (in this case the movement of materials), and was based on the collection of primary data, - since the vessels don't document their activities, and also because there are few studies related to the port of Parintins - through questionnaires applied to the vessels taking part in the research, with questions about their operations, internal handling and the movement of materials in the port. The questionnaire is qualitative and quantitative, with both a measured analysis in numbers and an inductive analysis by the researcher to interpret the relationship between reality and the object of study (DALFOVO; LANA; SILVEIRA, 2008).

The questionnaires were administered at the port of Parintins, and were answered by the owners of the boats, as they contain information with more restricted access, by the crew responsible for the operation of the boat and by those responsible for the transportation of cargo, due to their constant work and knowledge of the activity. This application began in March 2015 and ended in April of the same year, covering five of the seven boats in the municipality of Parintins that transport passengers and goods on the Parintins/Manaus/Parintins stretch.

Data was only collected from boats belonging to the municipality of Parintins, so that the flow of materials would be more visible. Of these boats, only 70% were interviewed, due to the fact that the owners and crew were absent or traveling with the boat when they weren't on duty, which requires a lot of attention. As each boat leaves the municipality on different days, it was necessary to obtain data on their departure and arrival at the port, which was obtained through informal inquiries at travel agencies, so all the boats could be approached. In order to protect the image and integrity of the boats, they have been referred to as boats **A**, **B**, **C**, **D** and **E**.

For information on the port of Parintins, its characteristics and the activities it carries out in terms of material handling, an unstructured interview was conducted with the port administration, which was recorded on audio and transcribed for better analysis. Additional information was obtained by means of an interview, recorded in notes, with the Port Authority, at the Brazilian Navy agency located in the town itself.

From the data collected, a database was built for later tabulation. To tabulate the quantitative data, Microsoft Office Excel was used for a more detailed analysis and the construction of graphs and tables. The qualitative data was analyzed one by one and compared with the reality of the municipality.

Results and discussion

In order to present the research objectives in a clear, succinct and organized manner, the results have been divided into four topics, each containing a part of the materials handling process.

Vessel operability

The boats used to transport goods and passengers in the municipality of Parintins are generally characterized according to Table 1 below:

Table 1: Vessel Characteristics

BOAT	VESSEL SIZE (METERS)	CAPACITY LOAD (TONS)	PASSENGER CAPACITY (UNIT)	NUMBER OF CREW MEMBERS
A	51	826	615	20
B	31	200	226	13
C	40	150	338	16
D	30	111	156	14
E	40	150	330	13
AVERAGE	38	287	333	15

Source: Field research results

The vessels have an average length of 38 meters from bow to stern, an average cargo capacity of 287 tons and an average passenger capacity of 333 people. Vessel **A** stands out among the others, both in terms of size and capacity. However, the size and capacity of the vessels do not affect travel time, as they have engines with the same power, with the outward journey from Parintins to Manaus taking more than 20 hours and the return journey from Manaus to Parintins taking between 17 and 20 hours, oscillations caused by the geospatial conditions inherent in the region. Although they use the same route for their journeys, the outward leg has a longer completion time due to the fact that the journey is up the Amazon River, and the return leg has a shorter completion time because it is down the river. Table 1 also shows the number of crew members working on the boats, who are certified professionals with a maritime license, which is a requirement of the Brazilian Navy, and auxiliaries.

The average turnover of a trip varies greatly according to the route and season. All the boats said that during the festive periods in the municipality of Parintins, such as Carnival, the folklore festival, the feast of the patron saint Nossa Senhora do Carmo, and on long holidays, such as Holy Week, Fatherland Week, among others, Turnover is higher and there is a preference for transporting passengers rather than goods, although 80% of the boats consider that most of their profits come from transporting goods, due to the location of the municipality of Parintins, since the available modes are only river and air. Vessel **B** considers that most of its profits come from transporting passengers because it considers this business to be more profitable and less problematic, since it has already experienced several unpleasant situations when it comes to transporting goods.

Table 2: Vessel turnover

BARC O	ONE-WAY BILLING (PASSENGERS)	Return BILLING (PASSENGERS)	Invoicing (LOAD)	IDATurnover (CHARGE)
A	R$ 15.000,00	R$ 10.000,00	R$ 0,00	R$ 30.000,00
B	R$ 5.000,00	R$ 2.000,00	R$ 0,00	R$ 3.000,00
C	R$ 3.000,00	R$ 5.000,00	R$ 0,00	R$ 10.000,00
D	R$ 3.000,00	R$ 4.000,00	R$ 0,00	R$ 6.000,00
E	R$ 9.000,00	R$ 3.500,00	R$ 0,00	R$ 12.000,00
MEDIUM	R$ 7.000,00	R$ 4.900,00	R$ 0,00	R$ 12.200,00

Source: Field research results

Based on common periods (outside of the high season), the average earnings for a round trip, as shown in Table 2 (above), is an average of R$ 7,000.00 for passenger transportation on the outward leg and R$ 4,900.00 for the return leg, while the average earnings for goods transportation is R$ 12,200.00 for the return leg. All the vessels said they didn't make any profit from transporting goods on the outward leg, but by observing the loading of goods, they did ship some small parcels, furniture, household appliances, among others. When the interviewees were asked about the transportation of this small amount of goods, they said that it happens sporadically and that's why they didn't consider it in the questionnaire.

When questioned about the fact that they make negligible profits from transporting goods on the outward stretch, the answer was unanimous: all of them said that the municipality of Parintins doesn't produce anything that the state capital needs. Although there are some small industries, their products are only distributed in Parintins and in some neighboring municipalities, which are not part of the route taken by the boats.

All the boats claim to obey the fare stipulated by the general price list of the Merchant Navy, which is readjusted every year. However, in the municipality of Parintins there are 7 boats that do the Parintins/Manaus/Parintins stretch and another 21 boats from municipalities in the state of Pará that dock at the port of Parintins, which also transport passengers and goods to the capital, causing competition between the boats, where whoever has the lowest price will have a greater number of cargoes transported and may have an increase in turnover.

As a result, boat owners report that they feel obliged to significantly reduce ticket prices in order to ensure that their boats remain in this very competitive market.

Boats **C**, **D** and **E** exempt children up to the age of 3, minors up to the age of 10 and senior citizens over the age of 60 from paying 50% of the fare. Vessel **B** exempts children under the age of 1 from paying the fare, children aged between 1 and 5 pay a fee of 20 Reals and children aged between 6 and 13 and the elderly aged 60 and over only pay 50% of the fare. Vessel **A** exempts children up to the age of 5 from paying the full fare, but from the age of 6 onwards, only the elderly over the age of 65 receive a 50% discount on the fare, with one caveat: in order to receive the discount, the elderly person must declare an income of less than one minimum wage. Vessel **A** was the only one to offer a discount to people with disabilities, since if they can prove their disability they only pay 50% of the fare.

The prices charged for the goods are not set out in a table, giving the ships freedom to set their own prices, so we understand why the biggest profits for the ships come from transporting goods. Vessels **A**, **C**, **D** and **E** use the number of volumes transported and the packaging required for the goods as criteria for setting freight rates. Vessel **B, on the** other hand, only takes into account the quantity of volumes transported, since it does not invest in its

13

vessel for the transportation of goods, as it opts for the transportation of passengers as its predominant service.

We will understand more about the issue of packaging goods and other matters that deal with the internal services of ships, with regard to the transportation of goods, in the next topic.

Internal Movement of Vessels

The process of transporting materials requires both agility and careful handling. Rosa (2007) explains that packaging is the main key to preserving the goods being transported, so there is a great need to keep products in suitable places so that there is no damage or loss to those transporting them. When we bring in the reality of the municipality's boats, we take a brief look at the business of transporting goods, where it can be seen that the contracting of this transportation comes from the receiving companies, in other words, the companies in the municipality of Parintins buy products manufactured in the state capital and are responsible for the costs of transporting the goods.

All the vessels have at least one area for the specific packaging of goods, which would be a sector for the transportation of smaller parcels or parcels of up to three volumes. Among them, vessels **A** and **C** are the only ones that have a refrigerator available for the proper stowage of goods that require greater care, given their perishability, and we observed the transportation of yogurts, meats, cold cuts, among others. The rest of the non-perishable cargo is stowed in the holds and on the first deck of the ships.

The vessels unanimously stated that the most transported goods are non-perishable foodstuffs, household appliances and electronics. As vessel **C** has a large meatpacking plant and transports large numbers of cold cuts on its voyages, and vessel **A** transports a large number of vehicles, the vessels sought to emphasize that they frequently transport these goods, so they were

15

singled out from the other vessels.

Rosa (2007) points out that even if all forms of loss, damage or violation of goods are analyzed and methods to combat these accidents are put into practice, such as proper packaging and stock control, there must always be a reserve to cover the costs of these damages. Vessels **A** and **B** say they do not have any form of insurance or liability for losses, violations or damage to the goods being transported, while vessels **C**, **D** and **E are** only liable for the loss of the goods and will replace them in the event of an accident. On vessels **A**, **C** and **D**, these claims occur sporadically and on vessels **B** and **E they are** more uncommon, according to the owners.

In the process of storing the goods, all the vessels proved to be very careful, since in the freight business not only the transportation of the goods is taken into account, but also the quality of the service provided. In a scenario where all vessels provide the same service and have equivalent prices, the quality of the service provided becomes a differentiator in the consumer's choice of company to carry out the transportation. To better understand the quality factor, we have the example presented by Novaes (2004) where a shipment of yogurt is being transported from one city to another by a truck driver and, in order to minimize fuel costs, the truck driver turns off the refrigerator. When he delivers the package, because it is sealed, the receiver of the goods has no way of checking that the product is properly preserved and receives it as normal. A few days later, after buying a yogurt from this batch, a consumer notices that the product has a different color and smell, due to improper storage. The customer will certainly seek a refund of the amount spent on the product, or even, in the case of consumption, potentially have an allergic reaction or other problem, which could lead to compensation as a result.

In this context, it can be seen that the biggest losers would be the receiving companies, or the manufacturing companies, both in terms of financial damage and reputational damage (image), since the name (brand) and where it was acquired will always be used to narrate the fact, but when the error is detected, companies tend to negotiate their freight services with another carrier. Looking at this example, we can see that even though the truck driver transported the goods and delivered them on time, he ended up not providing the quality of service expected. The truck driver ended up losing both the lot he was transporting and the continuity of the service, so we can see the importance of quality as a determining factor in the consumer's choice of who will provide the service.

When asked about the difficulties they encounter in transporting goods, the interviewees differed in their answers. Vessel **A** firmly stated that claims (losses, damages and breakdowns) are the biggest difficulty they encounter. The fact that they are not responsible for losses, damages or breaches creates a major problem for the vessel, but the vessel says it informs its clients about the conditions for contracting the service. Vessels **B** and **D** pointed out that their main difficulty is the financial return. As well as the fact that there are countless vessels that transport goods, the companies that contract this service impose a price below the market price, and due to the great competition, the vessels feel forced to accept the price set by the service contractors. Ship **B** also highlighted inflation as a major villain in the business of transporting goods, since prices have been rising frequently, especially the price of fuel, and yet the prices charged for freight remain intact. Vessels **C** and **E** say that they have no difficulties when it comes to transporting goods, as they have areas set aside for proper packaging and with a large capacity, and their costs for carrying out this service are covered by their turnover.

Material Handling in Porto

The main responsibility of the boats is to pack and transport the goods. Loading and unloading is carried out by stevedores, employees of the distribution companies and employees of the receiving companies, together with the boat's crew. All the processes are done manually since the boats don't carry large quantities of goods, making it unnecessary to use machines to move materials around the port of Parintins. All the boats interviewed provide their crew members with uniforms and personal protective equipment (PPE) to carry out their work, but what was observed is that even though they are provided with this equipment, many employees don't use it. The owners of the boats say that one or two of them do not use the protective equipment, but the employees are subject to verbal and written warnings if they fail to comply with this rule stipulated by the Brazilian Navy.

As we saw in the first topic, the boats in the municipality of Parintins only transport goods on the Manaus/Parintins stretch, so the analysis of the loading of goods onto the boats will take place at the Manaus Moderna port, located in the center of the state capital, next to the Municipal port. Figure 1 shows how goods are loaded onto the vessels.

Figura 1 : **Ship loading flowchart**

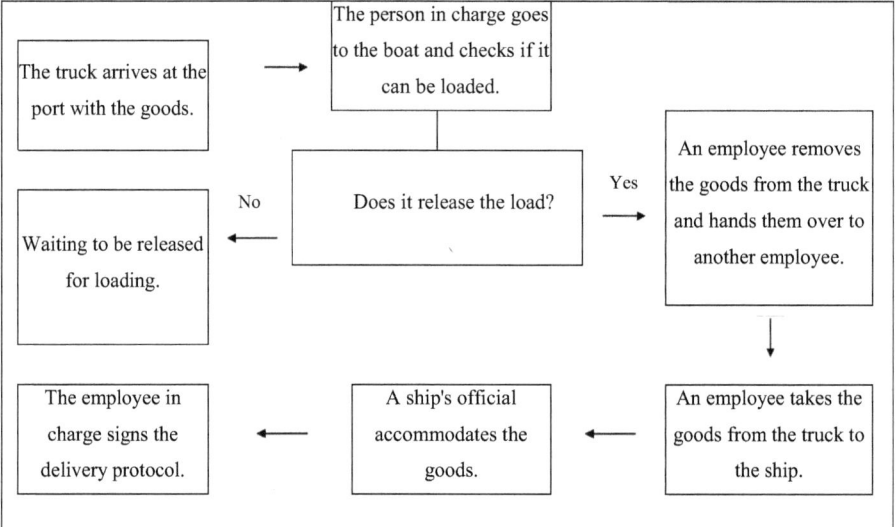

Source: Field research results

The distributors (suppliers of the goods) are responsible for loading the goods onto the ship. When they arrive with the goods, which are usually brought in by truck, the employee in charge goes to the ship to confirm that the goods have been loaded. When they are not cleared, due to overloading, lack of staff or some other unforeseen event, the goods await clearance in order to continue with the loading process. When the load is released, the employees unload the truck, carrying the boxes, bags and other packages on their shoulders, heads or backs, all by hand. When they get off the truck with the goods, the employees go down the staircase and take the iron raft to the

20

ship, where the crew receives the goods, also by hand, and quickly accommodates them. The entire loading process is monitored from the moment the truck leaves until it enters the ship by the employee responsible for the goods, and the process of entry and accommodation is monitored by a ship's employee. At the end of the loading process, the employee responsible for the goods and the person in charge of the ship sign the invoice from the distribution company and the ship's internal control protocol. From then on, the ship becomes responsible for the goods, in accordance with each company's transportation policies.

The goods are unloaded at the port of Parintins, which can be understood by looking at Figure 2 below.

Figura 2 **Flowchart for unloading goods from ships**

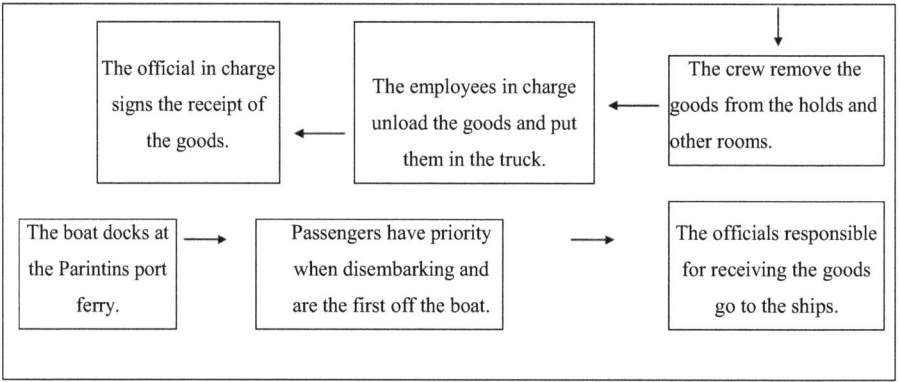

Source: Field research results

When boats dock at the Parintins port ferry, priority is given to disembarking passengers and their luggage, parcels and goods. Once the passengers have finished disembarking, the boat authorizes the unloading of goods. The officials responsible for this have to cross an iron bridge linking the port to the ferry to gain access to the boat. Unloading is done manually, where crew members take the goods out of the hold, or other space set aside for this purpose, and hand them over to those responsible for unloading, who load the packages manually from the boat onto the truck. When unloading is complete, the person responsible for receiving the goods signs the ship's control protocol and the receipt note from the distribution company, and the employee goes to the truck and drives the goods across the iron bridge to the final recipient.

The loading and unloading process in the port of Manaus Moderna and in the port of Parintins is carried out in an agile but manual way - in contrast to what is observed in the country's major ports, such as the port of Santos.

state of São Paulo. The vessels and employees responsible for the process work as a team and ensure the quality of the service, handling the goods with care to maintain the integrity of the products.

Port of Parintins and its Functionalities

The Port of Parintins is located in the center of the municipality, covering an area of 7,675m^2 and has been administered since 2006 by AHIMOC - Administraçâo das Hidrovias da Amazônia Ocidental, a federal authority linked to the Ministry of Transport. Vessels dock at a 150-meter-long, 15-meter-wide iron ferry, which is connected to the port's physical structures by a 65-meter-long iron bridge, with passage for vehicles and pedestrians. The Brazilian Navy agency in the municipality, in view of Art. 16, item II, of Law No. 9,537 of December 11, 1997, regulated through Ordinance 159/CFAOC of July 18, 2014 that the sum of all vessels and their cargoes moored at this iron ferry must not exceed the maximum limit of 1,250 tons, half of the actual capacity supported.

The port's responsibility with regard to the movement of materials is to facilitate the access of passengers and goods to the vessels in a safe and organized manner, overseeing the processes of entry and exit of goods and passengers. The port also supervises the crew of vessels, stevedores and other port workers, and if the administration finds irregularities such as failure to wear personal protective equipment, it can penalize the worker by banning them from entering the port to carry out their work. The port administration carries out this inspection, but it is common to find several workers without uniforms or safety equipment, and most of the time the warning is given verbally. Gildete Prado, the port's operational supervisor, says there is no need for the port's machinery and facilities to assist in the handling of materials, as the ships themselves opt for manual handling, due to its speed and low cost. The port's employees do not take part in the loading and unloading process on the ships, but the administration does have a table that keeps track of the quantity and type of goods the ships are carrying.

In response to the question about the lack of equipment for the handling process, such as machinery and warehouses, Gildete says that when the port was inaugurated in 2006, there was a small forklift for use in this process, the ships didn't feel the need to use this or any other piece of equipment to move materials, and because of its uselessness to ships in the context of the port of Parintins, the forklift was returned to the Ministry of Transport for relocation. Gildete says that the port has a small 35m warehouse^2 that is rarely used. In the case of ships that need to unload goods and continue on their way, when those responsible cannot unload the goods, the ships move the cargo to this small warehouse, When the receiving companies are willing to receive the goods, they pay a rental fee for the warehouse and sign the notes from the distribution companies and the port's internal protocols. However, Gildete emphasizes how rare these situations are, due to the complexity and bureaucracy of the process.

FINAL CONSIDERATIONS

When we talk about material handling, the issue of quality service is emphasized, both in order to obtain a financial return, minimizing potential losses with the replacement of goods, and in order to create an atmosphere conducive to customer loyalty due to the good service provided.

Despite the use of traditional and anachronistic methods for the movement of materials, it can be seen that all the agents involved in the movement process value the quality of service, both dockers and port operators.

We have seen that no matter how careful they are, there is a great possibility of these contingencies occurring because they don't use the most appropriate and efficient techniques for control and safety in storage and transportation.

The movement of materials is not carried out manually in the ports due to the lack of equipment or machinery, but because the ships in the municipality of Parintins have opted for this method because they believe it is the most agile and the most appropriate for the reality experienced here. In the same way, public bodies don't invest in the port of Parintins because of the municipality's lack of demand for services related to the transportation of goods, since the municipality has only small industries, and these don't offer products on a scale to meet the needs of the state capital. Equipping the port with machinery, warehouses and other apparatus to assist in the process of moving materials would be costly to the public coffers and would imply unnecessary expenses that would cause a poor return on that reality, and it is also worth noting that the vessels are only designed to perform services manually due to their physical structures.

Therefore, it can be seen that even in a scenario of great competition and supply of services on the market, the municipality's boats invest in the quality and agility of their services, because even though they carry them out in a more traditional and archaic way, it matches the municipality's demand for this activity.

References

ANDRADE, E. A. T. et al. ANALYSIS OF CARGO MOVEMENT IN A PORT OPERATION: A CASE STUDY. Rio de Janeiro, 2013.

ARAÙJO, F. H. C. B. BRAZILIAN PORT SYSTEM: EVOLUTION AND CHALLENGES. Florianópolis, 2013.

BRAZIL. Law No. 9,537 of December 11, 1997.

BURSZTYN, M.; DRUMMOND, J. A.; NASCIMENTO, E. P. HOW TO WRITE (AND PUBLISH) A SCIENTIFIC WORK: TIPS FOR YOUNG RESEARCHERS. Rio de Janeiro, 2010.

CAVALCANTE, R. M. F.; FONTINELLY, Y.; ROCHA, A. N. T. UMA RECONSTRUÇÂO DA HISTÓRIA DE PARINTINS ATRAVÉS DE RELATOS DE MORADORES ANTIGOS E DA LINGUAGEM FOTOGRÂFICA. Palmas, 2012.

DALFOVO, M. S.; LANA, R. A.; SILVEIRA, A. MÉTODOS QUALITATIVOS E QUANTITATIVOS: UM RESGATE TEÓRICO. Blumenau, 2008.

IBGE - Brazilian Institute of Geography and Statistics

FERREIRA, K. A; RIBEIRO, P. C. C. LOGÌSTICA E TRANSPORTES: UMA DISCUTÃO SOBRE OS MODAIS DE TRANSPORTE E O PANORAMA BRASILEIRO. Curitiba, 2002.

NOVAES, A. G. LOGISTICS AND DISTRIBUTION CHAIN MANAGEMENT: STRATEGY, OPERATION AND EVALUATION. 2 ed. rev. and current. Rio de

Janeiro: Campus, 2004.

PALM, P. R. THE OPENING OF THE AMAZON RIVER TO INTERNATIONAL NAVIGATION AND THE BRAZILIAN PARLIAMENT. Brasilia, 2009.

ROSA, A. C. TRANSPORTATION MANAGEMENT IN PHYSICAL DISTRIBUTION LOGISTICS: AN ANALYSIS OF OPERATIONAL COST MINIMIZATION. Taubaté, 2007.

SILVA, D. N. et al. THE MOVEMENT OF MATERIALS IN THE PORT OF MODERN MANAUS. Florianópolis, 2013.

SOARE, M. D. TRANSPORTATION MANAGEMENT. Coimbra, 2012.

VERGARA, S. C. PROJETOS E RELATÓRIOS DE PESQUISA EM ADMINISTRAÇÃO. 11 ed. Sâo Paulo: Atlas, 2009.

Lena Andrea Lima Muniz :

http://lattes.cnpq.br/9848606212073884.

PhD student in the Postgraduate Program in Economics (PPGE/UFPA), **Master** in Regional Development of the Amazon (UFAM), Specialist in People, Market and Technology Management (IFAM). **Graduated** in Economics (CIESA).

Graduated in Economics (CIESA) and studying Social Sciences (UFAM). She is a project economist for Banco da Amazônia, Suframa, Banco do Brasil and SEPLACT. Economic **consultant** at L. A. MUNIZ Consultoria e Projetos. She has teaching experience as a substitute **professor** at the Federal University of Amazonas (UFAM) and assistant professor at the Amazonas State University (UEA). She has experience in the field of Economics, with an emphasis on Regional and Environmental Economics, working mainly on the following subjects: income, social inclusion, socio-economic impacts, economic analysis and environmental valuation.

Academic background

2016

PhD in progress in POS GRADUATION PROGRAM

IN ECONOMICS.

Federal University of Para, UFPA, Brazil.

Title: Environmental valuation of fishing resources in the Macuricanâ

Complex/Am,

Advisor: Marcelo Bentes Diniz.

Grant recipient: Coordinaçâo de Aperfeiçoamento de Pessoal de

Nivel Superior, CAPES, Brazil.

2010 - 2012

Master's Degree in Regional Development (CAPES Concept 3).

Federal University of Amazonas, UFAM, Brazil.

Title: SUBSIDIES FOR AN ENVIRONMENTAL VALUATION STUDY

DA LAGOA DA FRANCESA NO MUNICIPIO DE PARINTINS/AM,Year

obtained: 2012.

Advisor: SYLVIO MARIO PUGA FERREIRA.

Co-supervisor: ADEMIR CASTRO E SILVA.

Grant recipient: National Council for Scientific and

Technology, CNPq, Brazil.

Keywords: Economic Development; Environment;

FRENCH LAGOON.

Major field: Applied Social Sciences

Large Area: Applied Social Sciences / Area: Economics.

Large Area: Applied Social Sciences / Area: Economics / Sub-area: Environmental economics.

Industry sectors: Scientific research and development.

2006 - 2007

Specialization in People, Market and Technology Management (Hours: 400h).

Federal de Educaçâo Tecnológica do Amazonas, FUNCEFET-AM, Brazil.

Title: People Management: Leadership and Organizational Behavior in Modern Institutions.

Advisor: Marcia Bacovis.

2008

Ongoing degree in social sciences.

Federal University of Amazonas, UFAM, Brazil.

1996 - 2007

Degree in Economics.

Centro Universitàrio de Ensino Superior do Amazonas, CIESA, Brazil. Title: Production Sector: a case study with the virtual company Sucesso.

Advisor: Rosana Zau Mafra.

1992 - 1994

Technical/professional course in Business Administration.

Senador Joâo bosco State School, EESJB, Brazil.

Research projects

2010 - 2012

SUBSIDIES FOR AN ENVIRONMENTAL VALUATION STUDY OF

LAGOA DA FRANCESA IN THE MUNICIPALITY OF PARINTINS/AM

Description: To subsidize public policies and studies that value the natural resources of the Lagoa da Francesa in Parintins/Am.

Situation: In progress; Nature: Research.

Members: Lena Andrea Lima Muniz - Coordinator.

2010 - 2011

'CHOICE MODELING AS A SUBSIDY FOR THE MANAGEMENT OF THE TARUMA-AÇU RIVER BASIN

Situation: In progress; Nature: Research.

members: Lena Andrea Lima Muniz - Coordinator.

2009 - Current

Community-based tourism chain as a strategy for

local development

Awards and titles

2014

GENTE QUE ACoNTECE - Outstanding Economist of the Year in the municipality of Parintins/AM, Promoter Frank Freitas.

Jalil Castro Dray : http://lattes.cnpq.br/9802867241096383.

BA in Economics from the Amazonas State University - UEA.

Specialist in Digital Marketing: Business and Strategy at the Pontifical Catholic University of Minas Gerais - PUC Minas.

He has a degree in Economic Science from the Amazonas State University (2015). He has experience in finance/banking, sales, the retail market and auditing.

Academic background : 2017

Ongoing specialization in Digital Marketing: Business and Strategies (Hours: 360h).

Pontifical Catholic University of Minas Gerais, PUC Minas, Brazil.

2017

Ongoing specialization in Strategic and Economic Business Management

(Workload: 360h).

Centro Universitàrio de Ensino Superior do Amazonas, CIESA, Brazil.

2010 - 2015

Degree in Economic Science.

Amazonas State University, UEA, Brazil.

Title: Movement of materials by boat in the municipality of Parintins/AM.

Advisor: Lena Andréa Lima Muniz.

2008 - 2010

High School (2nd grade).

Nossa Senhora do Carmo College, CNSC, Brazil.

Francisco   Werlen   da   Silva   Taveira   :

http://lattes.cnpq.br/2191141176634615

Bachelor in Administration from the Federal University of Amazonas - UFAM. (Organizer). He works in the areas of Human Resources Management, Public Administration and Psychology. He currently writes scientific articles for indexed national and international journals.

Graduated in Administration from the Federal University of Amazonas - UFAM (2017). He was Project Director at Parintins Jr - Consultoria Empresarial,

junior management company. He coordinated the course's 6th Academic Week. He was a student representative on the administration course, chaired the founding assembly of the first UFAM Jr Company in Parintins - AM, developed several extension projects where he held leadership positions, took part in research projects funded by the Amazonas State Research Support Foundation (FAPEAM) and served on various committees at the same university. He has completed various training courses at institutions, foundations and fairs of national and international renown and prestige, such as: International Amazon Fair (VII and VIII ? FIAM), BM&FBovespa, Fundaçâo Estudar, USP, UFAM, SEBRAE, SENAI, SENAC, CETAM, CIEE, Controladoria Geral da Uniâo (CGU), Câmara dos Dirigentes Lojistas do Amazonas (CDL-AM), among others.

Academic background :

2012 - 2016

Degree in Business Administration.

Federal University of Amazonas, UFAM, Brazil.

Title: Bolsa familia: aspects and contributions to quality of life. Supervisor: Pedro Marinho Amoêdo.

Further Education : 2014 - 2014

Inspection of Public Accounts (Hours: 4 hours). Federal University of Amazonas, UFAM, Brazil.

2014 - 2014

Career Management (Hours: 3 hours).

Nùcleo Brasileiro de Estàgios LTDA, NUBE, Brazil.

2013 - 2013

Basic Sanitation (Hours: 3 hours).

Federal University of Amazonas, UFAM, Brazil.

2011 - 2011

FINANCIAL ADMINISTRATION (Hours: 15h).

Support Service for Micro and Small Companies in Amazonas, SEBRAE/AM, Brazil.

2011 - 2011

Financial Mathematics I. (Hours: 20h).

Company-School Integration Center, CIEE, Brazil.

2011 - 2011

Financial Mathematics II. (Hours: 20h).

Centro de Integraçao Empresa - Escola, CIEE, Brazil.

2010 - 2010

FINANCIAL CONTROLS (Workload: 15h).

Support Service for Micro and Small Companies in Amazonas, SEBRAE/AM, Brazil.

2010 - 2010

BASIC ACCOUNTING. (Hours: 240h).

Technological Education Center of Amazonas, CETAM, Brazil.

2009 - 2009

SALES TECHNIQUES. (Workload: 30h).

National Commercial Learning Service - AM, SENAC/AM, Brazil.

2009 - 2009

LEARNING TO ENTERPRISE (Workload: 20h).

Support Service for Micro and Small Companies in Amazonas, SEBRAE/AM, Brazil.

2008 - 2008

RESEARCH METHODOLOGY. (Workload: 40h).

Technological Education Center of Amazonas, CETAM, Brazil.

2008 - 2008

AGRICULTURAL MANAGEMENT (Hours: 80h).

Technological Education Center of Amazonas, CETAM, Brazil.

2007 - 2007

Basic Informatics (Hours: 92 hours).

Technological Education Center of Amazonas, CETAM, Brazil.

Research projects : 2015 - 2016

Bureaucracy x efficiency at work: an analysis based on motivation theories at the Federal University of Amazonas Parintins Campus **2015 - 2016**

Bolsa Familia: aspects and contributions to quality of life

Extension projects :

2016 - 2016

Awakening community entrepreneurship

2016 - 2016

Academic Organizational Consulting

2016 - 2016

Vocational Test: Building a Path to the Academic Universe **2016 - 2016**

Administrative practices applied in Parintin's commerce: promoting sales techniques

2016 - 2016

Employability starts at school: young people ready for the future **2016 - 2016**

Academic Business Consulting: actions for entrepreneurial training

2016 - 2016

Managing the 4 P's: promoting the practice of marketing for artisans **2015 - 2015**

Learning Paths

2014 - 2014

Community-based Management for Sustainable Tourism

2013 - 2013

Agent of Change: An Alternative for Community Development that Starts with Me

Printed by Books on Demand GmbH, Norderstedt / Germany